BYTE ME AND OTHER RISKY BUSINESS

CREATING A CULTURE OF CYBER SAFETY

BY RAE WITCHER

Byte Me and Other Risky Business

Rae Witcher

© 2024 Rae Witcher

ALL RIGHTS RESERVED. This book contains material protected under International and Federal Copyright Laws and Treaties. Any unauthorized reprint or use of this material is prohibited. No part of this book, or use of characters in this book, may be reproduced or transmitted in any form or by any means, electronic or mechanical, including photocopying, recording, or by any information storage and retrieval system without expressed written permission from the author / publisher, except for review and educational purposes

To those seeking a little safety and solace

RISK ASSESSMENT IS ONE OF THE BEST TOOLS YOU CAN HAVE FOR SURVIVING AND, HOPEFULLY, EVEN THRIVING IN THE WORLD THAT WE'RE LIVING IN.

RISK ASSESSMENT IS A WAY TO ANALYZE POTENTIAL THREATS AND THE REPERCUSSIONS OF THOSE THREATS.

IT'S A LIKE A MAP IN YOUR BRAIN OF WHERE YOUR BOUNDARIES ARE, WHERE POTENTIAL HAZARDS MAY BE, AND HOW YOU MIGHT PROACTIVELY AND REACTIVELY RESPOND IN CERTAIN SCENARIOS

THE GOAL OF RISK ASSESSMENT IS TO FIGURE OUT WHAT RISKS AND REPERCUSSIONS YOU'RE OK WITH AND HOW TO ELIMINATE OR MINIMIZE RISKS YOU MAY NOT BE OK WITH THE CONSEQUENCES OF TAKING.

EVERYONE NEEDS TO ASSESS THEIR RISKS, BUT IT MAY BE ESPECIALLY PERTINENT TO THOSE WITH MARGINALIZED IDENTITIES AND THOSE WITH ALTERNATIVE LIFESTYLES.

WE CAN AND SHOULD ASSESS RISKS IN ALL AREAS OF OUR LIVES; WORK, SCHOOL, WITH OUR HEALTH, IN OUR RELATIONSHIPS, FRIENDSHIPS...

AND ESPECIALLY ONLINE

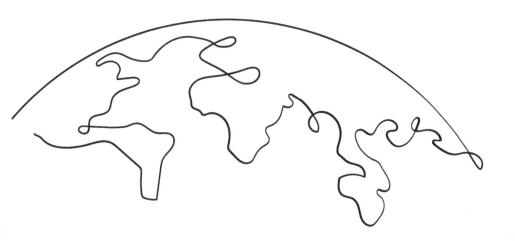

Does this all sound cliche and simple? Well, some of it is, but it can get complicated.

Online we can have multiple presences and personas. Some personas may be more public; like a work or resume website...

While other online personas may be more private or only for a closer circle of people to see ... or potentially even anonymous.

HOW DO WE BALANCE IT ALL? AND KEEP OURSELVES AND THOSE AROUND US SAFE?

REMEMBER, THE WORLD IS YOUR AUDIENCE

THE INTERNET IS VAST... AND OFTEN FOREVER

"WITH GREAT POWER COMES GREAT RESPONSIBILITY"

BE CAREFUL WHAT YOU POST. THINK ABOUT RISKS FACTORS SUCH AS...

- WHO MIGHT FIND YOUR CONTENT?

- WHAT THEY MIGHT USE IT FOR?

- COULD IT EXPLOIT YOURSELF OR OTHERS?

- IS IT SOMETHING THAT COULD INCRIMINATE YOU IN SOME WAY NOW OR IN THE FUTURE?

UTILIZE PRIVACY SETTINGS

YOU'RE IN CONTROL OF YOUR ONLINE AUDIENCES

YOU CAN KEEP A TIGHTER AND MORE SECURE CIRCLES ONLINE

AND CHOOSE WHAT IS APPROPRIATE FOR YOU AND YOUR RISK PROFILE ACROSS DIFFERENT PLATFORMS

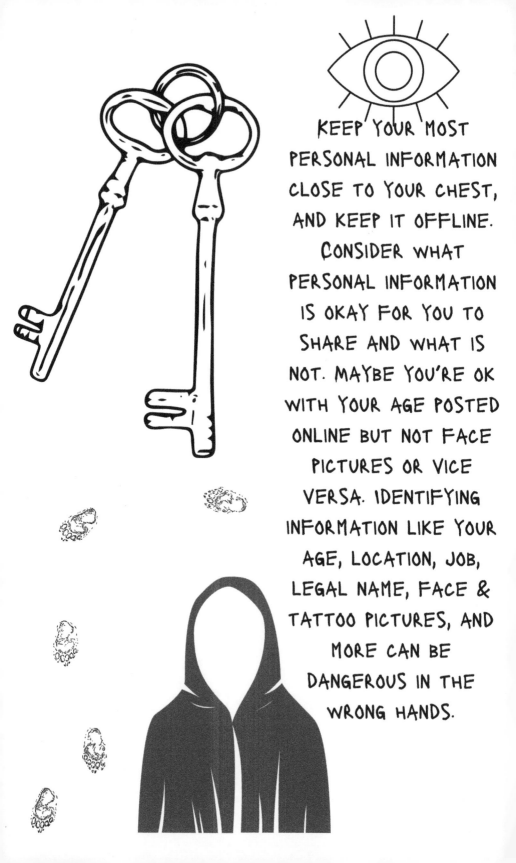

KEEP YOUR MOST PERSONAL INFORMATION CLOSE TO YOUR CHEST, AND KEEP IT OFFLINE. CONSIDER WHAT PERSONAL INFORMATION IS OKAY FOR YOU TO SHARE AND WHAT IS NOT. MAYBE YOU'RE OK WITH YOUR AGE POSTED ONLINE BUT NOT FACE PICTURES OR VICE VERSA. IDENTIFYING INFORMATION LIKE YOUR AGE, LOCATION, JOB, LEGAL NAME, FACE & TATTOO PICTURES, AND MORE CAN BE DANGEROUS IN THE WRONG HANDS.

BE CAREFUL OF WHO YOU ASSOCIATE YOURSELF WITH AND BEFRIEND ONLINE. STRANGER DANGER IS STILL A THING! MAKE SURE YOU HAVE A GOOD WAY TO VET PEOPLE OR MAYBE CONSIDER A RULE THAT YOU ALSO NEED TO HAVE MET THEM IN REAL LIFE TO BE THEIR FRIEND ON CERTAIN SOCIAL MEDIA SITES.

IT'S IMPORTANT FOR PEOPLE IN OUR LIVES TO KNOW WHAT RISKS WE ARE AND ARE NOT WILLING TO TAKE WHEN INTERACTING, COMMUNICATING, AND POSTING ABOUT EACH OTHER ONLINE.

IDEALLY, WE COULD ALL BE "OUT" ALL THE TIME AND BE AN OPEN BOOK, BUT THAT'S NOT ALWAYS SAFE IN EVERY SITUATION WE FIND OURSELVES IN. UNFORTUNATELY, WE NEED TO BE THINKING ABOUT AND TALKING TO THOSE IN OUR DAILY LIFE ABOUT HOW AND WHERE WE ARE "OUT" AS QUEER, KINKY, POLYAMOROUS, AND OTHER IDENTITIES THAT MAY NOT ALWAYS BE VISIBLE.

HERE ARE SOME QUESTIONS TO INSPIRE YOU AS YOU TALK WITH YOUR PARTNERS, FRIENDS, AND FAMILY ABOUT ONLINE RISK MANAGEMENT:

ARE YOU OK WITH ME POSTING PHOTOS OF YOU? SHOULD I ASK BEFOREHAND, IF SO? CAN I POST THEM IMMEDIATELY OR SHOULD WE WAIT A DAY OR TWO? SHOULD I BLUR OR CENSOR YOUR FACE OR BODY? CAN I TAG YOU?

CAN I POST ABOUT BEING AT CERTAIN LOCATION OR EVENT WITH YOU? DURING THE THE TIME WE'RE THERE? AFTER WE LEAVE ONLY? CAN I TAG YOU?

ALSO CONSIDER, ASKING QUESTIONS ABOUT WHAT PERSONAL INFO THEY ARE OK WITH ONLINE, SO YOU DON'T ACCIDENTALLY OUT OR OVERSTEP THE BOUNDARIES OF SOMEONE YOU LOVE.

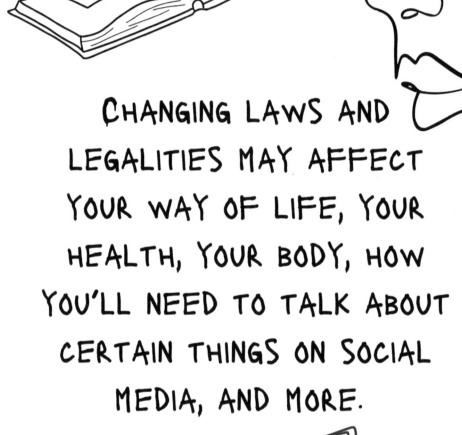

Changing laws and legalities may affect your way of life, your health, your body, how you'll need to talk about certain things on social media, and more.

IT IS VITAL TO KEEP UP WITH NEWS THE BEST YOU CAN IN A WAY THAT IS HELPFUL AND HEALTHY FOR YOU.

YOU MAY BE A NEWS HOUND AND LISTEN TO NPR, AND READ AN ONLINE LOCAL NEWSPAPER EVERY DAY. OR MAYBE IT'S OVERWHELMING FOR YOU, AND YOU JUST LOOK AT HEADLINES AND DIG INTO ARTICLES YOU FEEL MIGHT BE PERTINENT TO YOU. IT COULD ALSO LOOK LIKE HAVING A POINT PERSON IN YOUR FRIEND OR FAMILY GROUP WHO CAN FILL YOU IN ON IMPORTANT CURRENT EVENTS.

CHOOSE A WAY TO STAY INFORMED THAT WORKS FOR YOU. THE WORST THING YOU CAN DO IS NOT LOOK OR LISTEN TO ANYTHING. IT'S IMPORTANT TO STAY ALERT AND KNOW WHAT'S GOING ON, SO YOU CAN BE PREPARED AND REACT ACCORDINGLY. IGNORANCE IS NOT ALWAYS BLISS!

IF YOU HAVE A NEED TO POST ON SOCIAL MEDIA ABOUT SOMETHING POTENTIALLY RISKY, FOR WHATEVER REASON, CONSIDER USING CODE WORDS AND THINKING CAREFULLY ABOUT HOW MUCH INFO YOU DIVULGE.

AN EXAMPLE OF THIS IS THE RISE IN POPULARITY OF USING "SPICY" INSTEAD OF "SEXY" IN SOME SPACES TO MAKE WHAT YOU ARE TALKING ABOUT MORE PG OR SFW.

DURING THE PROHIBITION, THEY CALLED AN ILLEGAL DRINKING ESTABLISHMENT A "BLIND PIG."

YOU MIGHT BE FAMILIAR WITH SOME OTHER RECENT CODE WORD EXAMPLES, TOO, SUCH AS CAMPING OR CORN.

MEDIA LITERACY IS IMPORTANT!

Don't believe everything you read on social media, in news sources, or even from people you know. Ahead are some quick ways to begin to evaluate what you consume online.

HERE ARE A FEW EXAMPLES OF HOW TO QUESTION THE AUTHOR AND THE SOURCE OF THE CONTENT YOU'RE CONSUMING:

- WHO IS THE AUTHOR?

- IS AN AUTHOR LISTED ON THE ARTICLE OR WEBSITE?

- IS IT A REPUTABLE, WELL KNOWN SOURCE?

- ARE THEY AN EXPERT IN WHAT THEY ARE SAYING OR HAVE THEY INTERVIEWED OR QUOTED EXPERTS?

- DO THEY HAVE SOMETHING TO GAIN BY POSTING THIS?

- WHAT IS THEIR PURPOSE?

WHEN ANALYZING ONLINE INFORMATION, CONSIDER SEEKING ALTERNATIVE VIEWPOINTS FROM MULTIPLE SOURCES

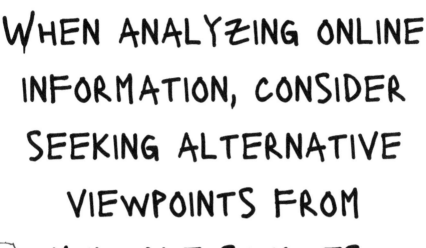

IF WHAT THEY ARE POSTING IS TRUE AND UP TO DATE, THERE ARE LIKELY MORE NEWS SOURCES AND OTHERS POSTING ABOUT IT. CHECK OTHER SOURCES OUT.

⚠ WARNING

STOP AND THINK BEFORE YOU POST

PAUSE BEFORE RESHARING A VIRAL POST OR TYPING OUT SOMETHING YOU HEARD WITHOUT FACT CHECKING. REMEMBER THAT THE MOST COMMON AND CONVINCING FALSE INFORMATION HAS A SLIVER OF TRUTH IN IT. MISINFORMATION SPREADS FAST AND CAN LEAD TO A LOT OF DAMAGE AND DISTRACT PEOPLE FROM REAL ISSUES AT HAND.

THIS BOOK IS NOT A COMPLETE GUIDE FOR HOW TO BE SAFE ONLINE. IT'S MEANT TO SPARK EXTRA THOUGHT AND CARE ABOUT YOUR INTERACTIONS ON THE INTERNET, AND IT IS ALSO MEANT TO BE A CONVERSATION STARTER. I ENCOURAGE YOU TO GO THINK CRITICALLY AND DO YOUR OWN DUE DILIGENCE SURROUNDING THESE TOPICS. THE BIGGEST GOAL IS TO HELP YOU TAKE CARE OF YOURSELF AND OTHERS.

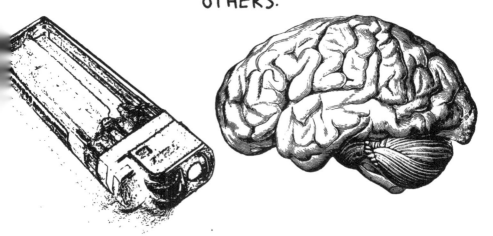

ABOUT THE AUTHOR

Rae is passionate about queer and trans rights, and they invite you to visit raewitcherbooks.com for more info.

www.ingramcontent.com/pod-product-compliance
Ingram Content Group UK Ltd.
Pitfield, Milton Keynes, MK11 3LW, UK
UKHW051350020125
453058UK00031B/225